FAST CARS

Extreme machines, packed with power

igloobooks

Published in 2013
by Igloo Books Ltd
Cottage Farm
Sywell
NN6 0BJ
www.igloobooks.com

SHE001 0913
2 4 6 8 10 9 7 5 3 1
ISBN 978-1-78197-919-8

Written by Robin Brown

Printed and manufactured in China

FAST CARS

Extreme machines, packed with power

CONTENTS

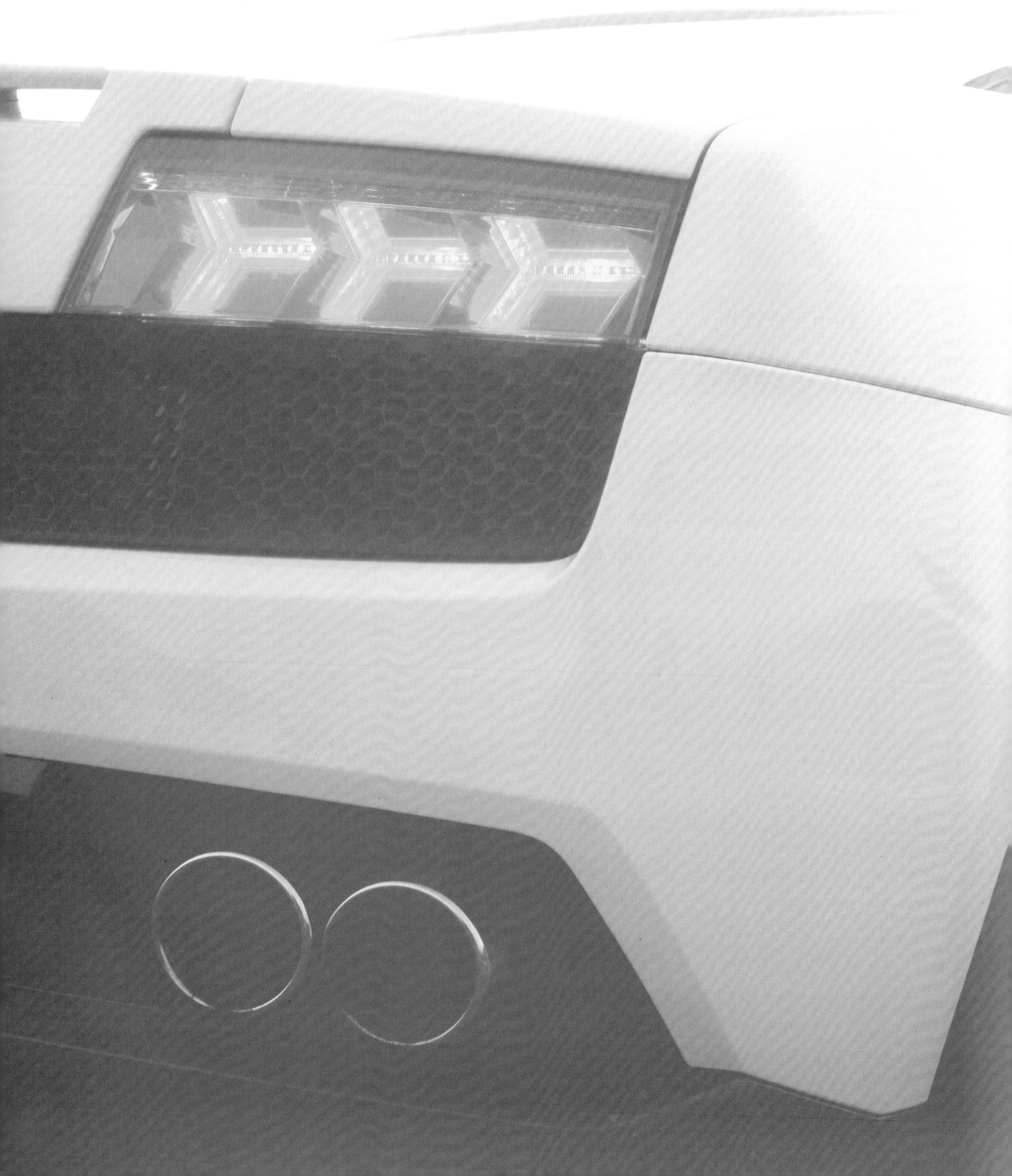

INTRODUCTION

It's extraordinary that the top speed of the world's fastest production car is the best part of 200mph faster than many legal speed limits of Western roads. For many owners of the world's most powerful supercars and hypercars the chance to make the most of their wheels might only come rarely - at the track or a journey through Germany, with its limitless Autobahnen.

It begs the questions as to why these cars even exist, why people buy them and why they're so desirable. For car manufacturers there exist huge PR benefits to building the fastest car in the world, but the technological advances that building such a car - and overcoming the accompanying obstacles - brings are significant too. As with motorsports, the advances in technology gleaned through producing these wickedly fast machines often filters down into high-volume road cars.

But there's a common reason as to why car-makers and car-buyers are entranced by speed: the simple love of cars and the desire to push the envelope. Some manufacturers eschew raw speed - prioritising driving dynamics, luxury or a combination of several factors. Yet Bugatti, SSC, Koenigsegg and others continue to battle it out for the crown of the fastest car in the world. Why? For the same reasons given by Mallory in retort to why climbing Everest was so important. Meeting the challenge - besting it, and achieving what was previously thought impossible.

Building a car that can travel at speed of over 250mph – much faster than a Formula One car – is an extraordinary technical challenge. Power required increases exponentially at speeds above 200mph thanks to aerodynamic drag.

So too does cooling and heat venting. Airflow over and under the car becomes a delicate balance between slipperiness and preventing the car from taking off. Fuel economy plummets to the point that miles-per-gallon are registered in barely whole numbers. And tyres operate at the very limits of the forces they can withstand.

The Veyron has, essentially, two V8 engines in tandem, with 16 cylinders and four turbochargers. Most cars have one radiator, the Veyron has 12. It' fuel pump capacity is eight times greater than most cars and it consumes the same amount of air in one minute as the air consumed by a man in four days.

That these fastest cars can hit those speeds while offering music players, satellite navigation, climate control and adjustable seats – all the creature comforts of an executive sedan – is so incredible it's almost laughable.

In their way these fastest cars in the world are less comparable to everyday road cars than they are to the flagships of modern speed, technology, inventiveness. The Flying Scotsman. Bluebird. Concorde. Yet they also represent one of the fundamental challenges that define us as a race. To be higher, faster, stronger. There are very good reasons to build the fastest car in the world, but the one that unites those who make cars and those who admire them is one of the most simple instincts; the desire to go faster.

FAST CARS
180-190
MPH

PORSCHE 911
CARRERA 4S

Porsche surprised everyone with the
911 Carrera 4S - a supercar that added
all-wheel drive to the 911 template.

While that may raise eyebrows - the 911's reputation as something of an untamed rear-wheel drive beast lends itself to expressive driving - there have been 911s in the past that send power to all four wheels.

The 911's unusual rear-mounted engine set-up makes for a singular challenge for drivers: that's the thrill of taming the Porsche supercar, but it poses unique challenges too - the spectre of oversteer haunting the inexperienced driver.

The obvious benefit of all-wheel drive is that torque is sent to all four wheels and, with almost 400bhp on tap, that's not a bad thing. In slippery conditions the all-wheel drive set up - capable of sending 100% of power to the front axle - offers significant security.

While that might suggest that the Carrera 4S has its edges smoothed off, this is still a supercar that can hit almost 190mph and sprints to 62mph in 4.5 seconds.

That's courtesy of a 394bhp 3.8-litre flat six engine through a slick seven-speed double-clutch autobox that aids fast starts, plus plenty of low-down pull from 440Nm of torque. Sport and Sport Plus setting firm up the suspension and throttle responses - as well as boosting the engine's throaty soundtrack.

The 911 has often been called the thinking man's supercar; with the 4S it could also be called the everyday supercar. Only this daily drive tops out at a startling 185 mph.

SPECIFICATION

MANUFACTURE DATE	2012	ENGINE	3.8-litre flat-six petrol
WIDTH	1,852 mm	TRANSMISSION	Six-speed manual
HEIGHT	1,303 mm	0-62 MPH	4.5 seconds
LENGTH	4,491 mm	POWER OUTPUT	394 / bhp
MAXIMUM TORQUE	440 / nm	BRAKES	4-piston, aluminium fixed monobloc calipers with, cross-drilled, ventilated discs
MAXIMUM SPEED	185 mph	SUSPENSION	McPherson strut suspension at front LSA multi-link at rear

MOSLER
MT900S

Transported straight from the track – and with only a few minimal adjustments from a genuine racer – the Mosler MT900S is lightweight and very fast. Topping out at 190mph, the Mosler gets very fast extremely quickly – to 60mph in a frightening 3.1 seconds, breaking the 100mph barrier in 6.6 seconds.

The MT900S uses a supercharged 5.7-litre V8 from Chevrolet, which puts out 435bhp in a carbon-aluminium set-up. This lack of weight is the secret to the Mosler's eye-watering acceleration – the power-to-weight ratio approaches an impressive 500bhp-per-ton.

American-based Mosler Automotive is owned by Warren Mosler, a financial guru with a serious passion for things fast and four-wheeled. The transmission is a Porsche 911 GT3-sourced six-speed gearbox or the Hewland six-speed sequential 'box that's a remnant from the track car.

The 435bhp 5.7-litre Corvette-sourced V8 engine develops maximum power at 5,800 rpm and there's also 542Nm of torque on tap that's accessible at ferociously short notice.

As a result there's very little that's polite or refined about the Mosler. The flipside of owning a stripped-out racer is that there are no mod cons, the engine noise intrudes massively into the cockpit and the cabin is basic. Entry into the car is via gullwing doors over a thick sill; the driver sits very low down in the cockpit too.

Steering is remarkably direct but very heavy – another nod to the Mosler's heritage - and the suspension, while not

bad for a race car, is fairly stiff, meaning that the MT900S is far from ideal for a jaunt to the shops.

However, for a car that mixes the best of the track with the usability that means it can be used on the road, the Mosler is a strong, blisteringly quick, package.

SPECIFICATION

MANUFACTURE DATE	2005	ENGINE	5.7-litre LS6 V-8
WIDTH	1,998 mm	TRANSMISSION	Six-speed manual
HEIGHT	1,041 mm	0-62 MPH	3.1 seconds
LENGTH	4,730 mm	POWER OUTPUT	435 / bhp @ 5,800 rpm
MAXIMUM TORQUE	542 / nm @ 4,800 rpm	BRAKES	AP 6-piston front calipers, 378mm ventilated front disc AP 4-piston rear calipers, 355mm ventilated rear disc
MAXIMUM SPEED	190 mph	SUSPENSION	Double wishbones at front and rear

ASTON MARTIN
DB9

The iconic DB9 is a grand tourer that pays tribute to former owner Dave Brown, with all the hallmarks of an Aston Martin – it's cool, elegant and sleek. But it can also travel at speeds nearing 200mph.

The DB9's 6.0-litre V12 develops 470bhp, but it's the 600Nm of torque and its impressive pull from low revs that set the DB9 apart as something special. It takes 4.8 seconds to hit 60mph and the top speed is 190mph – however it's the way that power is transmitted so smoothly through either a six-speed manual or six-speed automatic Touchtronic gearbox, which can be controlled using wheel-mounted paddles for changing gear.

The Aston Martin 2+2 is most at home on smooth, flat A-roads, where it is poised and has glue-like grip going around corners, but it's refined at even high speeds, making it perfect for long punts down motorways, freeways or the Autobahn. The Volante version loses the roof but there's no accompanying drop in performance.

The DB9 is refined and poised – as the James Bond connection demands – and inside, the car has more toys that Q might pack it with. Alongside the usual navigation and media additions there's a raft of safety kit from Volvo (the only clue that the DB9 shares some limited similarities with its then-stablemates Ford, Volvo, Jaguar and Land Rover) and even a tracker so that police can pick up the car should it be acquired by bad guys, though sadly no ejector seat.

The Aston Martin DB9 is a potent combination of power and elegance – combining long range touring ability and fine sports car handling. As such, the latest Dave Brown is classic Aston Martin.

SPECIFICATION

MANUFACTURE DATE	2008-2012	ENGINE	748-valve 6.0-litre petrol V12
WIDTH	1,017 mm	TRANSMISSION	Six-speed manual or touchtronic
HEIGHT	1,270 mm	0-62 MPH	4.6 seconds
LENGTH	4,710 mm	POWER OUTPUT	470 / bhp
MAXIMUM TORQUE	600 / nm	BRAKES	Brembo carbon-ceramic brakes
MAXIMUM SPEED	190 mph	SUSPENSION	All-round independent double-wishbone suspension

FAST CARS
190-200
MPH

ASTON MARTIN
DBS V12

Look familiar? If you're wondering where you might have seen the Aston Martin DBS on celluloid recently it's the car that James Bond rolls in Casino Royale. And, this being an Aston, it has history.

The original, a 325bhp 4.0-litre straight-six, was introduced in 1967 and can be seen in the movie On Her Majesty's Secret Service. It's also an extension of the DB9, with only a few outward cosmetic tweaks that are aimed at improving high-performance stability and reducing kerb weight.

The DB9 may not be lacking in power and performance, but for those who want a harder edge from their Aston Martin there's the DBS. This 6.0-litre V12 petrol engine is boosted to return 512bhp, meaning that 60mph passes in just over four seconds – and the coupé keeps going all the way up to 191mph.

That's partly due to engine tweaks, but there are also carbon fiber body panels and brakes that save weight. Despite the DBS's rougher edge, the ride comfort is not compromised but the Aston feels a little more nimble than the DB9, thanks to the lower kerbweight.

There's oceans of torque from as little as 2500rpm that allows for those fast sprints, but the character of the car is very much iron fist, velvet glove. The DB9 is a wonderful tourer and cruises smoothly at motorway speeds.

There are plenty of visual cues inside the car – the Handbuilt In England inscription on the kickplates as you open the door says it all. This is a classically elegant British interior given a modern makeover. The two rear seats have been removed to make way for more luggage space so there's a definite practicality here too; a high-quality stereo, satnav from Volvo and Bluetooth connectivity provide some gadgets worthy of Bond too.

The DBS may be 'just' a harder, faster, meaner DB9, but it does evoke that old Aston machismo of the Vanquish S. It is the ultimate Aston Martin.

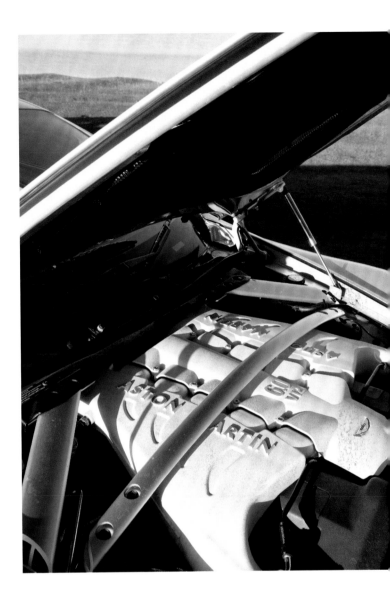

SPECIFICATION

MANUFACTURE DATE	2007-12	ENGINE	6.0-litre V12 petrol engine
WIDTH	1,905 mm	TRANSMISSION	Six-speed manual (optional 6-Speed Automatic)
HEIGHT	1,280 mm	0-62 MPH	4.3 seconds
LENGTH	4,722 mm	POWER OUTPUT	512 / bhp
MAXIMUM TORQUE	569 / nm	BRAKES	Front: 398 mm ventilated and drilled brakes with 6-piston alloy monobloc calipers. Rear: 360 mm ventilated and drilled brakes with 4-piston alloy monobloc callipers
MAXIMUM SPEED	191 mph	SUSPENSION	Adjustable double wishbone adaptive suspension

NISSAN
GT-R SKYLINE

Nissan has had an on-off relationship with supercars over the years, from the first Skyline back in 1969 through to the 1990 model that defined Japanese sports cars for a generation.

Fast forward 15 years and the new GT-R appeared – a 911-baiting sports coupe with plenty of performance and a low price tag. Any questions regarding Nissan's claims for the GT-R to be classed a supercar are surely dispelled by the performance figures: a huge 534bhp from a thundering 3.8-litre twin-turbo V6 go to all four wheels via a a six-speed twin-clutch gearbox and raft of active driving aids.

Astonishingly, it reaches 60mph in just 3.0 seconds, courtesy of the huge reserves of power and torque – and electronic trickery able to transmit. A launch control also aids these super-fast starts and steering-wheel mounted paddles mean that changing gear is seamless. The stability system can be configured to suit road and track driving.

The GT-R's external styling isn't subtle. It's big, chunky and aggressive but the car's apparent unwieldiness belies a stiff chassis that makes it extremely nimble when manoeuvring.

SPECIFICATION

MANUFACTURE DATE	2007	ENGINE	3.8-litre twin-turbo V6
WIDTH	1,895 mm	TRANSMISSION	Six-speed automatic dual clutch
HEIGHT	1,369 mm	0-62 MPH	3.0 seconds
LENGTH	4,656 mm	POWER OUTPUT	550 / bhp
MAXIMUM TORQUE	632 / nm	BRAKES	Brembo 6-piston aluminium monoblock calipers and 380mm drilled floating discs at front. 4-piston aluminium monoblock calipers with 380mm drilled floating discs at rear
MAXIMUM SPEED	193 mph	SUSPENSION	Bilstein damptronic fully adjustable suspension

With all of that power and torque on tap – 632Nm in the latter instance – the GT-R has excellent brakes with very little fade and awesome stopping power.

The dashboard has a vast array of instrumentation providing data on performance such as steering input degrees and cornering G-forces – but there's plenty of pleasant trim inside and arguably room for four and a good boot at 315 litres.

Just in case there are any doubts about the usability of the Nissan coupé, there's also cruise control, a good stereo system, and electrically adjustable and heated leather-trimmed seats as standard.

Still, Nissan has built a car built for performance first and foremost, with an engine that defies logic with the oceans of power and torque it can develop. With acceleration and out-and-out speed of 193mph the GT-R shames many more expensive supercars and dispels any lingering badge snobbery with its undeniable ferocious turn of pace.

AUDI
R8 V10

The Audi R8 V8 is hardly lacking in firepower, but for those seeking a little more Lamborghini in their Audi supercar there's the R8 V10. Packing the Gallardo's 5.2-litre V10 petrol engine, the R8 V10 develops 543bhp, which propels the R8 to 60mph in 3.9 seconds and tops out at almost 200mph.

There's not just power, but torque too. The engine revs to 8,700rpm so gearing is extremely flexible and acceleration formidable. The V10 Plus gets the new S tronic seven-speed auto, whose superfast gear changes make the sprint possible in just 3.5 seconds. It also gets a lowered and stiffened fixed-rate sports suspension for even sharper handling, while ceramic brakes – standard on the V10 Plus - gives stopping ability that is almost brake-fade free.

Handling on the standard model is designed to be comfortable, with Comfort Magnetic-fluid damping as standard smoothing out the ride, but handling is tight, flexible and communicative due to rear-wheel drive with the back-up of torque distribution to all four wheels should it be required, courtesy of the quattro four-wheel-drive system.

Coupe and soft-top Spyder models are both available, with little drop-off in drivability in the convertible.

All models come with LED daytime running lights and LED rear indicators but the V10 gets special Y-design 19-inch alloy wheels and more pronounced side-blades. There's also satellite navigation, Audi Music Interface with integrated Bluetooth, heated seats and all-LED lights.

In the supercar stakes, the addition of extra power and torque means the R8 V10 faces off against the likes of the Porsche 911 and Aston Martin Vantage, but the likes of the Ferrari 458 Italia and stablemate Lamborghini Gallardo are also on the radar of the Audi supercar.

SPECIFICATION

MANUFACTURE DATE	2008	ENGINE	5.2-litre V10 petrol
WIDTH	2,029 mm	TRANSMISSION	Seven-speed auto S tronic
HEIGHT	1,252 mm	0-62 MPH	3.9 seconds
LENGTH	4,431 mm	POWER OUTPUT	543 / bhp
MAXIMUM TORQUE	530 / nm	BRAKES	Wave brake discs, internally ventilated, 8-piston brake calipers at front; 4-piston at rear
MAXIMUM SPEED	196 mph	SUSPENSION	Sports suspension with dynamically tuned spring and damper combination

BMW
ALPINA B5 S

Based on the BMW M5, the Aplina B5 S is one of the fastest BMWs in the manufacturer's history; capable of phenomenal speed for a donor car more apt for motorway and Autobahn cruising.

Where BMW has traditionally eschewed forced induction and automatic gearboxes, the B5 S makes use of both – meaning 197mph is possible in this large executive four-door sedan, putting it among the fastest of its kind in the world. To put that into perspective, from a standing start the Alpina B5 S can theoretically beat the Aston Martin DBS to a kilometre.

The S version is powered by the BMW 4.4-litre supercharged V8 but this one puts out 530bhp through a six-speed automatic gearbox controlled via two buttons on the back of the steering wheel.

Despite the car's weight, the Alpina S has a frightening turn of pace courtesy of a staggering 725Nm of torque that's noticeable throughout the rev range. A limited-slip differential keeps the rear wheels in check.

20-inch alloy wheels also ensure the Alpina is able to transmit all that power, but there's also help from the suspension, BMW's Electronic Damper Control and the ability to change suspension settings depending on requirements. Choose the Sport button and throttle responses sharpen up significantly, revealing the B5 S's trackday potential.

SPECIFICATION

MANUFACTURE DATE	2005	ENGINE	V8, 4398cc, supercharged biturbo
WIDTH	1,860 mm	TRANSMISSION	Eight-speed auto, rear-wheel drive
HEIGHT	1,464 mm	0-62 MPH	4.6 seconds
LENGTH	4,899 mm	POWER OUTPUT	523 bhp @ 5500 rpm
MAXIMUM TORQUE	535 lb ft @ 4750 rpm	BRAKES	374mm and 370mm front to rear with automatic brake drying
MAXIMUM SPEED	197 mph	SUSPENSION	Alpina Sport Suspension

However, Comfort and Normal settings make the B5 S a potential daily drive too – preferring an element of refinement to the manic M5. The B5 S provides an alternative to the M5 for drivers seeking a more usable car, with a more pliant ride than the BMW donor car.

The Alpina arguably takes the edge off the M5, but it still packs a phenomenal amount of power; it remains a four-door family car than can manage almost 200mph.

FERRARI
612
SCAGLIETTI

The 540bhp, rear-drive Ferrari 612 Scaglietti was claimed to be the fastest four-door in the world when it went on sale. While Bentley may have had something to say about that, the official top speed is an impressive 199mph.

That's courtesy of a 532bhp 5.7-litre V12 that sent 588Nm of torque to the rear wheels and propelled the 612 to 60mph in just over four seconds. Power delivery is languid and the plentiful low-end torque is progressive all the way up to 5250rpm.

The rear-mounted gearbox shifts fluently, especially in auto mode, while driver-dialled dynamic settings mean the 612 can be driven as a luxury grand tourer or legitimately be taken onto the track. Hit Sport mode and the 612's electronic aids back off.

Transmissions include a six-speed F1 single-clutch automated manual and Ferrari's manettino – and F1-inspired dial on the steering wheel that allows the driver to select one of five different driving modes – was added to later models.

Meanwhile speed-sensitive steering that's light at high speeds and heavier around town to boost everyday drivability, despite the car's whopping 4902mm length.

The 612's cabin is roomy, the dashboard a winning mix of analogue and digital dials and there is a reminder of Ferrari heritage in a plaque listing Ferrari's five recent F1 world constructor championship titles.

The four seats are firm, supportive and electrically adjustable and do genuinely allow for four passengers. The 612 may defy easy categorization, but with an equipment list that includes the likes of xenon headlights, an adaptive suspension system, a power-closing boot, parking sensors, navigation system and Bose audio system with Bluetooth wireless connectivity and a 15GB music server the car is best thought of as a performance grand tourer.

The 612 Scaglietti's motorsport underpinnings ensure that the Ferrari can match similar grand tourers for performance, yet the fundamentally unhurried nature of the car also ensures the 612 is a genuine potential daily drive.

SPECIFICATION

MANUFACTURE DATE	2004-11	ENGINE	5.7 L Tipo F133F V12
WIDTH	1,956 mm	TRANSMISSION	Six-speed manual or Six-speed F1A semi-auto
HEIGHT	1,344 mm	0-62 MPH	4.3 seconds
LENGTH	4,902 mm	POWER OUTPUT	532 / bhp
MAXIMUM TORQUE	588 / nm	BRAKES	8-piston calipers and 380mm ceramic discs front; 4-piston calipers and 380mm ceramic discs rear
MAXIMUM SPEED	199 mph	SUSPENSION	Double-wishbone suspension's adaptive damping

BENTLEY CONTINENTAL GT

The Bentley Continental GT is a stunning coupé that blends classic Bentley DNA with contemporary design and modern technology – offering a combination of supercar performance and handcrafted luxury.

The Continental GT is perhaps the ultimate Grand Tourer, boasting then-revolutionary suspension when the coupe hit the roads in 2003, including Intelligent Continuous Damping Control that constantly monitors the car's attitude and poise, adjusting the suspension hundreds of times a second to alter ride stiffness depending on circumstances and road quality.

The Continental GT was all-wheel drive, with the car's vast amounts of power and torque distributed through all four wheels, with a 40:60 split power ratio for added security in difficult conditions and improved cornering – an uprated Electronic Stability Control was also added.

The 12-cylinder 6.0-litre W12 engine was the most compact 12-cylinder engine in the world at the time and capable of running on petrol, bioethanol or a combination of the two.

With its power output raised to 567bhp and torque up to 700Nm through an eight-speed Quickshift transmission, the Conti GT can go from a standstill to 60mph in just 4.4 seconds and reach a top speed of 200mph.

All Bentley models are famously handmade at the manufacturer's Crewe factory. Over 80 per cent of the entire cabin is trimmed with soft-touch leather, while the GT has a full range of wood veneers, cool-touch metals and deep-pile carpets.

SPECIFICATION

MANUFACTURE DATE	2003	ENGINE	6-litre W12 twin-turbocharged Flexfuel
WIDTH	2,227 mm	TRANSMISSION	Eight-speed Quickshift
HEIGHT	1,404 mm	0-62 MPH	4.4 seconds
LENGTH	4,806 mm	POWER OUTPUT	567 / bhp
MAXIMUM TORQUE	700 / nm	BRAKES	Vented front and rear disc brakes
MAXIMUM SPEED	200 mph	SUSPENSION	Air springs with Continuous Damping Control (CDC)

FAST CARS
200-210
MPH

FERRARI
F40

When the Ferrari F40 was launched in 1984 it was the fastest supercar in the world, topping out at 201mph.

Designed to celebrate the 40th anniversary of Ferrari car production, hence the F40 name, the supercar was a replacement for the popular 288 GTO but soon became one of the most iconic Ferrari cars of all time.

The Ferrari F40 is a particularly stripped-back car with a focus on lightweight architecture – carbon fibre and aluminium are used unsparingly throughout – and its aerodynamic design makes use of the 2.9-litre V8 engine developing 471bhp.

At 4500rpm, the Ferrari F40 delivers 577Nm of torque and everything about the drive train was upgraded from the Ferrari 288 GTO it replaced, including improvements to its displacement, compression ratio and even turbochargers.

Everything about the F40 is aimed at delivering a focused driving experience and the car has been shorn of any extras that do not contribute to the on-road dynamics.

Renowned for providing a visceral driving thrill like no other, the Ferrari F40 uses a mid-engine, rear-wheel drive setup and, while the 0-62mph sprint time is an impressive 3.7 seconds, it is the manner of the delivery that makes this one of the best supercars ever made.

G920 CLK

SPECIFICATION

MANUFACTURE DATE	1987-1992	ENGINE	2.9-litre V8 petrol
WIDTH	1,980 mm	TRANSMISSION	Five-speed manual
HEIGHT	1, 130 mm	0-62 MPH	3.7 seconds
LENGTH	4,430 mm	POWER OUTPUT	471 / bhp
MAXIMUM TORQUE	557 / nm	BRAKES	13.0-in. vented discs/ 13.0-in. vented discs
MAXIMUM SPEED	201 mph	SUSPENSION	Wishbones with coil springs over adjustable Koni shock absorbers. Front and rear anti-roll bars. Electronically adjustable suspension as an option

Driving the F40 is an incredible experience; the suspension is stiff and steering responsive at higher speeds and the feeling of speed is amplified by the feel of every bump in the road. Famed for its ability to catch out the inexperienced driver once it is up to speed, the Ferrari F40 is a brute of a supercar.

For many the outrageous supercar looks, including that huge rear spoiler and road-hugging stance, and ferocious driving performance put the Ferrari F40 at the top of the pile when it comes to supercars.

Ferrari went on to build over 1,300 F40s, all painted red, and as a result it is not the rarest supercar the brand has produced. However, it was the last commissioned by Enzo Ferrari and probably the best-loved model to come from the Ferrari stable.

LAMBORGHINI GALLARDO LP560-4

The Lamborghini Gallardo LP560-4 is an improved version of the brand's most recognisable car and delivers awe-inspiring performance and power.

Before its 2008 launch, the Gallardo name already had a reputation for fearsome performance where power outweighed refinement for a full-blooded driving experience.

All sharp lines and aggressive style, the Gallardo design has been unchanged, on the surface at least, for many years. However, the latest iteration to use the Gallardo name does boast some subtle tweaks including a more aerodynamic body and weight loss of around 20kg over the previous generation.

The Lamborghini Gallardo LP560-4 added more power to the Gallardo courtesy of a 5.2-litre V10 engine that delivers 552bhp. This provides a top speed of 202mph and a 0-62mph sprint time of 3.7 seconds.

Power goes to all four wheels and with 398lb of torque at 6500rpm this is necessary to distribute the sheer power of the V10 powerplant.

The Lamborghini has a reputation as a car that is brash and wild but the LP560-4 does offer subtle upgrades to reduce the chance of losing control in corners. This includes a revamped suspension to give the car more stability in corners and smoother suspension.

However, the throaty roar of the V10 engine remains and continues to be the main aspect drivers of this car take away from the experience. More refined than ever, it rises to a crescendo as the car moves through the gears ensuring the driver makes no mistake about the level of power on offer.

Inside the Lamborghini Gallardo LP560-4 the car benefits from the quality delivered by parent group Volkswagen. Meanwhile, an 18 per cent cut in CO2 emissions and a pedestrian-friendly front end point to a more responsible, practical supercar.

While that may be the case the new refined Lamborghini Gallardo LP560-4 is still a superb supercar in every sense. Its razor-sharp lines are sure to stir something within every car fan and the roar of the engine is still one of the most thrilling sounds on the road today.

SPECIFICATION

MANUFACTURE DATE	2008	ENGINE	5.2-litre V10 petrol
WIDTH	1,900 mm	TRANSMISSION	Six-speed manual or six-speed E-gear
HEIGHT	1, 165 mm	0-62 MPH	3.7 seconds
LENGTH	4,386 mm	POWER OUTPUT	542 / bhp
MAXIMUM TORQUE	540 / nm	BRAKES	365 x 34 mm (14.4- x 1.33-inch) steel ventilated rotors (front) and 356 x 32 mm (14.01- x 1.25-inch) ventilated rotors (back).
MAXIMUM SPEED	202 mph	SUSPENSION	Double-wishbone construction on the front and rear

FERRARI
F50

How do you follow a car like the Ferrari F40? For the Italian car maker, the only option was to add more power and a rawer driving experience.

E nter the Ferrari F50, a distinctive supercar that delivers racing performance and an ostentatious design that guarantees driving one will attract plenty of attention.

Described by Ferrari as the closest thing to a road-going F1 car, the F50 is an incredible machine that was limited to just over 300 units, creating a rarity and high price that puts it out of reach of most supercar fans.

While the F40 was a highly stylised design, the F50 is heavily influenced by F1 cars with a road-hugging stance, huge rear spoiler and sweeping curves.

The influences from the peak of motorsport include a carbonfibre monocoque that provides enough integrity to cosset the driver in the event of an accident. In the case of the F50, Ferrari knew it would need to be secure enough for road use.

On the road, the F50 has a reputation for a being an unruly powerhouse. The reputation is fitting; the Ferrari F50 packs in 520bhp from the V12 engine, which itself was inspired by the brand's F1 cars of the 1990s.

If that was not enough, the F50 does not come with power assistance for the brakes and steering giving the car a more involved – and harder to control – drive.

The Ferrari F50 is quicker than the F40 it replaced. The F1-style improvements mean a top speed of 207mph is possible and the 0-62mph sprint time is just 3.7 seconds.

Its 4.7-litre V12 engine churns out an incredible 750bhp and 471Nm of torque at 6500rpm and this power, along with a raw driving experience, is often levelled as a criticism of the brash F50.

However, there is no doubt the car delivers a unique driving experience and the addition of a removable hard top means the sound of the V12 engine can be enjoyed in the open air.

The Ferrari F50 was first introduced in 1995, the brand's 50th anniversary, and production lasted just two years.

SPECIFICATION

MANUFACTURE DATE	1995 -1997	ENGINE	4.7-litre V12
WIDTH	1,986 mm	TRANSMISSION	Six-speed manual, limited slip differential
HEIGHT	1,120 mm	0-62 MPH	3.7 seconds
LENGTH	4,480 mm	POWER OUTPUT	750 / bhp
MAXIMUM TORQUE	471 / nm	BRAKES	Brembo cross-drilled & ventilated cast iron discs, 4 piston aluminium Brembo calipers. No ABS.
MAXIMUM SPEED	207 mph	SUSPENSION	Rose-jointed unequal-length wishbones. Front and rear anti-roll bars

FERRARI
599 GTB

The Ferrari 599 GTB is a supercar that matches F1-style technology with a typically emotive design that represents the car maker's signature.

The two-seat Ferrari 599 GTB was introduced in 2007 as a replacement for the 575 and delivers even more performance than its predecessor.

Often referred to as the Fiorano after the Ferrari race track that its ride and handling were honed on, the 599 GTB has a reputation as one of the best-loved Ferrari gran turismo models.

Capable of reaching 205mph, it uses a 6.0-litre V12 engine producing 661 bhp and owners get a choice of six-speed manual gearbox or a six-speed 'F1 Superfast' option.

The F1 Superfast gearbox is lifted from the brand's successful F1 cars and delivers ultra-fast gear changes via steering wheel paddles. Ferrari estimates gear changes take just 100ms in performance situations.

Despite being the most powerful Ferrari ever sold when it arrived, the Ferrari 599 GTB is notable for its controlled, comfortable ride as a result of F1-inspired technology.

Ferrari's Magneride suspension adapts the car to suit driving conditions and the F1-trac control system is designed to read handling data and change the brakes and suspension accordingly. This allows the car to feel comfortable in straight lines but sharp around corners.

As a result the rear-wheel drive supercar is perfect for taking onto a track and the sheer power and noise coming from the engine bay will deliver pure driving pleasure.

Ferrari has developed the exhaust and cabin to improve the quality of the sound being delivered into the cabin via a tube feeding the intake sound towards the driver and passenger The Ferrari 599 GTB was eventually replaced by the Ferrari F12 Berlinetta but many will class this as one of the most technically advanced supercars to ever grace the road.

An optional package called the HGTE package is also available for the 599 GTB which improves handling by delivering stiffened springs, a rear anti-roll bar and tweaks to the Magneride system for a more track-based driving feel.

SPECIFICATION

MANUFACTURE DATE	2007	ENGINE	6.0-litre / V12
WIDTH	1,962 mm	TRANSMISSION	Six-speed manual or F1 Superfast gearbox with steering-mounted paddles
HEIGHT	1,336 mm	0-62 MPH	3.3 seconds
LENGTH	4,665 mm	POWER OUTPUT	661 / bhp
MAXIMUM TORQUE	620 / nm	BRAKES	13.9 x 1.3 in (front) and 12.9 x 1.1 in (rear)carbon ceramic brakes
MAXIMUM SPEED	205 mph	SUSPENSION	Magneride suspension capable of adapting to road conditions. F1-Trac manages data and adjusts settings accordingly

MASERATI
MC12

The Maserati MC12 is a two-seat supercar with more than a little in common with the Ferrari Enzo. In fact, the MC12 is actually based on an Enzo platform but comes with a revamped design.

It took an extensive makeover for the Maserati MC12 to emerge in its current guise and nearly all parts have been replaced. As a result the MC12 feels like a unique car – and a limited production run of just 50 mean it is also an incredibly rare car.

To transform the Enzo, Maserati extended the wheelbase and stretched out the car for better aerodynamics including the addition of a rear spoiler to boost down-force at higher speeds.

The two-door supercar has a mid-rear layout using a 6.0-litre V12 engine taken from the Ferrari Enzo. The engine delivers 600bhp at 7200rpm and 655Nm at 5500rpm and helps to propel the car to a top speed of 205mph.

Weight distribution is 41 per cent front and 59 per cent rear while the use of carbon fiber and other alloys have kept weight to a minimum on the MC12.

The sequential six-speed gearbox is operated by paddles and the car roars through the lower gears to deliver supreme acceleration – it can reach 62mph in just 3.8 seconds from standing.

The size and power of the Maserati MC12 means it is one of the more challenging cars to drive even with traction control turned on. The lack of rear window can hinder visibility as well – but there is the option of removing the roof to turn it into a convertible.

Originally designed for the track, the Maserati MC12 has had to undergo some tweaks to ensure it can be used on the road. The cabin is obviously influenced by its racing heritage with a flat-topped steering wheel, carbon fiber and leather surfaces and sports seats – but the cabin does lack some comforts such as a radio or sound system.

The Maserati MC12 is essentially a track car that has undergone some small tweaks to allow it to be road legal and all 50 editions are available in a single colour choice; blue and white.

SPECIFICATION

MANUFACTURE DATE	2004	ENGINE	6.0-litre / V12
WIDTH	2,100 mm	TRANSMISSION	Six-speed Maserati Cambiocorsa
HEIGHT	1,205 mm	0-62 MPH	3.7 seconds
LENGTH	5,143 mm	POWER OUTPUT	600 / bhp
MAXIMUM TORQUE	655 / nm	BRAKES	Brembo front brakes with six-piston calipers and the rear brakes with four-piston calipers
MAXIMUM SPEED	205 mph	SUSPENSION	Independent wishbone suspension with push-rod actuated dampers

FORD
GT

The Ford GT is a muscular, two-seat supercar based on the iconic GT racers of the 1960s and built in limited numbers.

Only 5000 Ford GT models were built between 2005 and 2006 as Ford took on the supercar heavyweights of Ferrari and Lamborghini.

To do this Ford uses a 5.4-litre supercharged V8 matched to a six-speed manual gearbox. The engine outputs 530bhp at 6500rpm and 678Nm of torque at 3750rpm and delivers impressive performance statistics.

Reaching 62mph from standing takes just 3.2 seconds and in just 7.4 seconds the car can travel at 100mph. It goes on to achieve a top speed of 205mph to match many of its more illustrious rivals.

The mid-engine layout negates the need for traction control in the GT and the engine is matched to a six-speed transmission.

It would be easy to consider the Ford GT as a way of cashing in on one of Ford's most iconic models – the racing GT40s from the 1960s - but the GT is an excellent car in its own right.

Built using an aluminium space frame chassis as opposed to the carbon fiber used by rivals, the Ford GT has been designed with speed and safety in mind.

Ford has designed the GT in the spirit of its iconic American muscle cars and amount of grunt on offer testifies to the success of this theme. The Ford GT delivers tremendous amounts of power and raw pace but can still be considered an everyday supercar.

Inside the cabin the clean, clear controls and comfortable seating area are a welcome change in the supercar segment but the car does have a sting in its tale when it comes to oversteer – something that will delight those who wish to take it on to a track.

Above all else the Ford GT is a car that is to be seen in and the level of exterior detail, iconic Ford racing stripes and distinctive, box-like rear end means the Ford GT remains an extremely popular supercar.

SPECIFICATION

MANUFACTURE DATE	2005 -2006	ENGINE	5.4-litre supercharged V8
WIDTH	1,950 mm	TRANSMISSION	Ricardo-sourced six-speed manual
HEIGHT	1,130 mm	0-62 MPH	3.2 seconds
LENGTH	4,640 mm	POWER OUTPUT	530 / bhp
MAXIMUM TORQUE	678 / nm	BRAKES	Four-piston aluminium Brembo calipers with cross-drilled and vented rotors at all four corners.
MAXIMUM SPEED	205 mph	SUSPENSION	Double-wishbone suspension design with unequal-length aluminium control arms, coil-over monotube shocks and stabilizer bars

LAMBORGHINI
REVENTON

The Lamborghini Reventon was the fastest roadster ever built when it arrived in 2009 in such limited numbers it also became one of the rarest of all time.

There is also a coupé version of the Reventon with similar design and performance figures but like the drop-top, numbers were limited to just 20 with an extra model being built for the Lamborghini museum.

T he fierce, angular design is unmistakably from the Lamborghini stable and creates the impression of a fighter jet as opposed to a drop-top supercar.

In fact, the design of the carbon fiber body was actually inspired by a fighter jet and the razor-sharp lines are a mix of traditional Lamborghini design and that of the EuroFighter jets.

The Reventon even has a jet-style G-force meter on the dashboard showcasing the forces the driver is being subjected to when under acceleration.

The engine is equally fearsome. It comes in the form of a 6.5-litre V12 engine with 690bhp on tap and 660Nm of torque at 6000rpm and delivers breathtaking performance figures.

Where legal, the Lamborghini Reventon can reach a top speed of 205mph and acceleration from 0 to 62mph takes just 3.4 seconds. The noise produced by the V12 Lamborghini engine adds an intensity to the driving experience.

Driving a Reventon is a challenge in itself because of the car's wide turning circle and immense amount of power that can leave the wheels spinning.

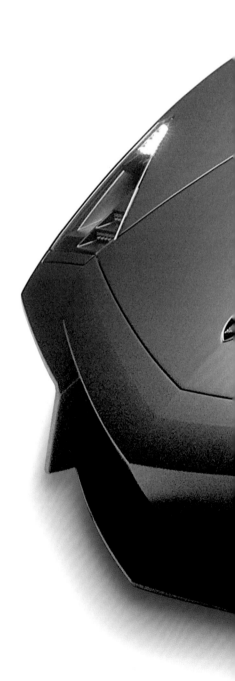

Lamborghinis are traditionally considered to be wilder than some of their more refined supercar rivals and the Reventon is a car tuned to provide an intense driving experience. The engine is mounted in front of the rear axle with the transmission in front, putting more of the weight towards the rear of the car.

Open one of the two scissor doors and the interior is typically luxurious with leather and aluminium adorning the seats and instrument panel. There are two sports seats and in the convertible version, advanced roll bars that pop up in a fraction of a second if the car is flipped over.

SPECIFICATION

MANUFACTURE DATE	2008	ENGINE	6.5-litre V12 petrol
WIDTH	2,058 mm	TRANSMISSION	Six-speed manual
HEIGHT	1,135 mm	0-62 MPH	3.4 seconds
LENGTH	4,700 mm	POWER OUTPUT	690 / bhp
MAXIMUM TORQUE	660 / nm	BRAKES	Carbon Ceramic brakes
MAXIMUM SPEED	205 mph	SUSPENSION	Double -wishbones, electronically adjustable hydraulic shocks, anti-roll bars, anti-dive and anti-squat characteristics

MCLAREN
MP4-12C

The McLaren MP4-12C was the car maker's triumphant return to road-legal cars after more than a decade focusing on its F1 team.

A major rival for the Ferrari 458 Italia, the McLaren MP4-12C has shunned the emotive design and heritage of its rival for a technical, precise supercar that demonstrates the cutting edge of supercar technology.

Everything from the carbon fiber composite chassis to the McLaren-designed engine has been carefully crafted to precise requirements.

The engine is a mid-mounted 3.8-litre twin-turbo V8 matched to a complex Seamless Shift seven-speed dual-clutch gearbox that boasts the ability to preselect the next gear by tapping the steering column-mounted paddles.

The engine develops 616bhp and can power the car to 62mph in a little over three seconds. There is 601Nm of torque on offer and 80 per cent of it is available at 2000rpm.

Top speed is a blistering 207mph and it is capable of braking from 124mph in just five seconds.

The McLaren MP4-12C has been designed with impeccable manners around a track with precise, responsive steering helped along by electronics capable of adjusting the car's systems to improve control.

As a result the McLaren MP4-12C is a car that can be driven very easily and the power coming from the engine can push the car forward like very few other cars on the market.

The McLaren's ability to corner is bolstered by a one-part carbon fiber chassis that is the first of its kind in a production car. A Proactive Chassis Control system adapts the car's output to cope with the incredible levels of power and torque from the engine.

McLaren was heavily influenced by its successful F1 program when it was designing the McLaren MP4-12C and a hydraulic anti-roll bar coupled with an advanced suspension setup comprising upper and lower wishbones helps to deliver a level of steering and control previously unseen on a supercar.

Inside the McLaren is surprisingly comfortable and good all-round visibility is a rarity in this segment and interior equipment includes Bluetooth, climate control and part-leather for the seats.

SPECIFICATION

MANUFACTURE DATE	2011	ENGINE	3.8-litre V8 petrol
WIDTH	2,909 mm	TRANSMISSION	Seven-speed manual dual clutch
HEIGHT	1,,199 mm	0-62 MPH	3.5 seconds
LENGTH	4,507 mm	POWER OUTPUT	626 / bhp
MAXIMUM TORQUE	601 / nm	BRAKES	Steel brakes as standard Ceramic brakes are an optional extra
MAXIMUM SPEED	207 mph	SUSPENSION	Adaptive suspension featuring hydraulic links to adapt to the road conditions

FAST CARS
210-230
MPH

LAMBORGHINI MURCIÉLAGO LP640

Introduced in 2006, the Lamborghini Murciélago LP640 model was designed as a spiritual successor to the Countach. The LP640 tag refers to the placement of the engine – Longitudinale Posteriore – and the number of horsepower the engine can develop.

The Lamborghini Murciélago LP640 also benefited from a larger front spoiler and larger air intakes, with a huge center-mounted exhaust. LED taillights, Hermera wheels and a glass-louvered engine cover were all new.

The Lamborghini V12 engine displaced 6.5 litres and power went up to 640bhp at 8000rpm. A six-speed gearbox incorporated a thrust mode on the optional e-Gear transmission, resulting in ultra-fast launches and a 60mph sprint time of 3.3 seconds. The quarter-mile took 11.2 seconds at 127mph.

Inside the Lamborghini Murciélago LP640 boasted a satellite navigation system, 140-litre trunk and the list of options was almost limitless, with bespoke interiors decided by buyers. Despite these touches, however, entry remained via roof-hinged doors and the V12 was another indication of the LP640's intent.

At the red line of 8000rpm the Murciélago has a fearsome roar, with 631bhp available from the 6.5-litre V12, which develops maximum torque of 660Nm at 5000rpm.

300 units were sold, though a Roadster version and a SuperVeloce model for the track followed. A Lamborghini Murciélago LP640 Versace was a limited-edition model available in either white or black: only 20 were produced as both coupés and roadsters while custom interiors were finished in two-toned Versace leather and included Versace luggage, driving shoes and gloves.

SPECIFICATION

MANUFACTURE DATE	2006	ENGINE	V12, 6496cc, 48v
WIDTH	2,045 mm	TRANSMISSION	Single-plate six-speed manual
HEIGHT	1,135 mm	0-62 MPH	3.3 seconds
LENGTH	4,580 mm	POWER OUTPUT	631 / bhp @ 8,000 rpm
MAXIMUM TORQUE	660 / nm @ 6,000 rpm	BRAKES	Porsche 380mm front x 355mm rear discs with four channel ABS
MAXIMUM SPEED	213 mph	SUSPENSION	Independent double-wishbone, anti-roll bar, anti-dive & anti-squat

PAGANI
ZONDA F

The Pagani Zonda F supercar paid tribute to founder Horacio Pagani and Formula One world champion race driver Juan Manuel Fangio. As such it was intended to show a commitment to lightness, performance and innovation and the Zonda F sported a logo, design concept and name dedicated to Fangio.

Built alongside its regular production model, the Zonda F is a special edition supercar which was refined to produce a more appealing supercar package. The changes resulted in a more lightweight, faster and more powerful car.

The resulting supercar is powered by a mid-mounted, longitudinal 7.3-litre V12 petrol engine with sequential multipoint injection that can output 594bhp and develop 780Nm of torque. The commitment to low kerbweight means extensive use of carbon fibre, titanium and aluminium.

Exhaust manifolds are designed in compliance with the Formula 1 standards and the use of the powerful Mercedes-AMG engine and lightweight engineering means a power-to-weight ratio of 529bhp/ton. Aerodynamics were also improved with the addition of a revised front end, new rear spoiler and more aerodynamic vents all around.

The Zonda F was equipped with an extra headlight and different fog lights at the sides, new bodywork and different side mirrors. Options included carbon and ceramic brakes developed in conjunction with Brembo, magnesium wheels and a chassis reengineered to improve rigidity and reduce weight.

The Zonda F sprints to 60mph in 3.6 seconds and 124mph (200kmh) in 9.8 seconds but can brake from 124mph to zero in 4.4 seconds, the awesome stopping ability courtesy of massive brake discs also available as optional ceramic discs to eradicate brake fade.

Production of the Pagani Zonda F was limited to 25 cars, though 25 examples were produced of the drop-top Zonda F Roadster.

SPECIFICATION

MANUFACTURE DATE	2005	ENGINE	V12, Mid-mounted, longitudinal V12 7.3-litre petrol engine with sequential multipoint injection
WIDTH	2,055 mm	TRANSMISSION	Six-speed manual gearbox, rear-wheel drive, limited-slip differential
HEIGHT	1,141 mm	0-62 MPH	3.6 seconds
LENGTH	4,435 mm	POWER OUTPUT	594 / bhp @ 6,200rpm
MAXIMUM TORQUE	780 / nm @ 4,000rpm	BRAKES	Ventilated carbon-ceramic discs, 380mm front and rear
MAXIMUM SPEED	214 mph	SUSPENSION	Double-wishbones, coil springs, dampers, anti-roll bar front and rear

PAGANI ZONDA CINQUE ROADSTER

With a production limited to only 5 cars, the Pagani Zonda Cinque Roadster is powered by a Mercedes AMG V12 engine producing 678bhp, hits 62mph from a standstill in just 3.4 seconds and tops out at 217mph. Stopping distances from 124mph were an eye-watering 4.3 seconds courtesy of carbon-ceramic brake discs.

The Zonda Cinque Roadster's twin-turbocharged engine transmits power through a sequential six-speed transmission and a range of electrical controls from Bosch including a traction control system to combat the acres of power and torque on offer.

Changes over and above the standard Zonda on the Cinque – Italian for five – include a stronger chassis, formed from a type of carbon fiber with threads of titanium woven into it, to stiffen the chassis when the roof is removed.

The striking Cinque features a remarkable rear too, with a redesigned exhaust that has also been completely redesigned and there are a number of additional carbon-fibre intakes and fins all over the car.

An adjustable suspension means that the car can be set up differently for a range of driving conditions, including fast-shifting track driving; the interior features carbon-fiber racing seats.

The chassis is a carbon-titanium monocoque for strength and lightness: a magnesium suspension, carbon-fiber brake discs and magnesium alloy wheels contribute to a dry weight of 1210kg – a massive 70kg lighter than the original Zonda S Roadster.

With only five ever built and an original price tag of over $2 million, you'll count yourself lucky to ever see one on the roads. Nevertheless the Pagani Zonda Cinque Roadster remains an irresistible example of hypercar exotica.

SPECIFICATION

MANUFACTURE DATE	2010	ENGINE	Twin turbocharged V12 Mercedes Benz AMG engine V12
WIDTH	2,055 mm	TRANSMISSION	Gearbox: Cima six-speed sequential gearbox
HEIGHT	1,151 mm	0-62 MPH	3.4 seconds
LENGTH	4,395 mm	POWER OUTPUT	678 / bhp
MAXIMUM TORQUE	780 / nm	BRAKES	380mm Brembo brakes in carbon-ceramic; self ventilated with hydraulic servo brake
MAXIMUM SPEED	217 mph	SUSPENSION	Double-wishbones, pull rod actuated coil springs, Ohlins adjustable shock absorbers, anti-roll bar

LAMBORGHINI
AVENTADOR
LP 700-4

The Lamborghini Aventador LP 700-4 is a two-door, two-seater supercar that replaced the Murciélago in 2011as the flagship model in the Lamborghini lineup. Needless to say, it's another Lamborghini named after a famed fighting bull – and the all-new V12 petrol engine is reassuringly powerful.

With a 6.5-litre V12 mated to a seven-speed ISR semi-automatic transmission, the Aventador is capable of a phenomenal 690bhp at 8,250rpm, with maximum torque of 690Nm at 5,500rpm. Those figures mean a top speed of 217mph and spine-crushing acceleration – 60mph in 2.9 seconds. The V12's power-to-weight ratio is 426bhp per tonne and the quarter-mile take a mere 10.6 seconds, by which time the Aventador is traveling at 137mph.

The single-clutch seven-speed semi-automatic is capable of shift in just 50 milliseconds while an all-wheel drive system from Haldex boosts traction and dynamic handling capacity with almost 700Nm of torque on tap. The Aventador is commonly held to be the most drivable Lamborghini ever, in contrast with the usual reputation of Lamborghini cars as brutally quick and dangerous for unwary drivers.

The Lamborghini flagship uses a carbon-fiber monocoque that is twice as stiff as the Murciélago even though it is lighter and more powerful. In terms of the Murciélago, the Aventador is slightly longer and narrower though it remains the same height.

The Aventador has a number of driver-specified features, such as a rear spoiler that can be set in three 3 positions depending on speed and drive select mode; ESP/ ABS with different ESP characteristics; steering and differential managed by drive select mode with three modes.

Endlessly customisable inside, the Aventador boasts the startling looks and power that Lamborghini is known for – and marries something of the outlook of a grand tourer. It's the most complete sports car that Lamborghini has ever made.

SPECIFICATION

MANUFACTURE DATE	2011	ENGINE	6.5-litre V12
WIDTH	2,030 mm	TRANSMISSION	Seven-speed ISR Semi-auto
HEIGHT	1,136 mm	0-62 MPH	2.9 seconds
LENGTH	4,780 mm	POWER OUTPUT	690 / bhp @ 8250 rpm
MAXIMUM TORQUE	690 / nm @ 5,500 rpm	BRAKES	Dual hydraulic circuit brake system, 400mm 6-cylinder brake calipers at front, 380mm 4-cylinder brake calipers at rear
MAXIMUM SPEED	217 mph	SUSPENSION	Front and rear horizontal monotube damper with push-rod system

FERRARI
LAFERRARI

Not one hybrid hypercar, but two. With the
McLaren P1 unveiled in 2012, Ferrari followed
up shortly afterwards with LaFerrari, unveiled
at the 2013 Geneva Motor Show.

The car, also known by the codename F70, is a limited-edition petrol-electric supercar that uses a KERS-like Formula One boost system providing the highest power output of any Ferrari whilst decreasing fuel consumption by 40 percent.

The LaFerrari's V12 petrol engine displaces 6.3 liters and has a power output of 789bhp, supplemented by a 163bhp HY-KERS system that provides overboost similar to that of a turbocharger. The LaFerrari has a top speed of 217mph and a sprint time of under three seconds; with 190mph possible from a standing start in under 15 seconds.

The V12 is mid-mounted and mated to an F1 dual-clutch gearbox with power going to the rear wheels. The resulting high levels of torque reach 900Nm and the powertrain revs up to the 9,250rpm limit.

The hybrid supercar has a dry weight of just 1,255kg and is built on a carbon fiber monocoque structure developed with 27 percent more torsional rigidity and 22 percent more beam stiffness than the Enzo. Carbon ceramic Brembo discs provide the stopping power.

Active aerodynamics include a front diffuser, underbody guide vane, rear diffuser and rear wing – leading to the best aerodynamic efficiency of any Ferrari. Electronic wizardry has been ported from Ferrari's Formula One programme and include an F1 electronic traction control, stability control, a third-generation electronic differential and magnetorheological damping that adjust the ride depending on conditions.

Ferrari says that only 499 units of the supercar will be built, while styling will be undertaken in-house by Ferrari – the first prancing horse not to have any styling input from Pininfarina since 1951. Prices will start at around $1.3m.

SPECIFICATION

MANUFACTURE DATE	2013	ENGINE	6.3-litre V12 with electric motor and KERS
WIDTH	1,992 mm	TRANSMISSION	Seven-speed dual-clutch automated manual
HEIGHT	1,116 mm	0-62 MPH	3.0 seconds
LENGTH	4,702 mm	POWER OUTPUT	789 / bhp + 163 / bhp
MAXIMUM TORQUE	900 / nm	BRAKES	Carbon ceramic Brembo discs on the front (398mm) and rear (380mm)
MAXIMUM SPEED	217 mph	SUSPENSION	Double-wishbone front suspension, multi-link rear suspension

GUMPERT
APOLLO

The Gumpert Apollo is hardly a subtle supercar. One of the most striking fast cars in the world – and blessed with one of the more unusual names – the Apollo was conceived by former Audi manager and motorsport honcho Roland Gumpert and uses an Audi-sourced twin-turbo V8, with power output as high as 780bhp and top speed of up to 224mph.

The powerful V8 has 40 valves, updated rods and pistons to cope with the awesome power created by to turbochargers strapped onto the engine. Peak power arrives at 6800rpm while maximum torque of 597lb-ft is developed at 5000rpm.

The body, such as it is, is composed of fiberglass or carbon-fiber, so weight is kept to a minimum – the Apollo weighs a paltry 1100kg as a result, meaning a power-to-weight ratio of a staggering 583bhp per tonne with the lower-rated 641bhp model. Meanwhile the Gumpert's aerodynamics are so effective that it can theoretically be driven upside-down in a tunnel at the higher end of the speed band, such is the downforce created by the car's spoiler and splitter.

SPECIFICATION

MANUFACTURE DATE	2005	ENGINE	4.2-litre V8
WIDTH	1,998 mm	TRANSMISSION	Six-speed sequential manual
HEIGHT	1,114 mm	0-62 MPH	3.1 seconds
LENGTH	4,460 mm	POWER OUTPUT	641 / bhp
MAXIMUM TORQUE	809 / nm	BRAKES	380mm discs on all wheels
MAXIMUM SPEED	224 mph	SUSPENSION	Double-wishbone suspension with adjustable rebound and compression. It also has a front anti-roll bar and a titanium rear anti-roll bar

Doors hinge from the middle of the roof and the big wheels arches enter into the cabin. Despite the Apollo being built to be used on the road, the interior belies its track-day appeal, with a minimalist carbon fiber interior with buckets seats and rows of dials are designed to feed back information on the car's dynamics and performance.

Most Apollos come with a sequential stick for changing gear – another feature most frequently seen in cars designed to be used to their full potential.

While technically a road car, the Apollo's hyper performance puts it almost beyond supercar status. Its screaming acceleration, enormous power-to-weight ratio and massive top speed put it virtually a league of its own.

FAST CARS
230-260
MPH

P1

The McLaren P1 is a rarity – a hybrid supercar that uses a petrol-electric powertrain to attain speeds in excess of 200mph.

The concept car debuted at the 2012 Paris Motor Show and represents McLaren Automotive's long-awaited successor to the legendary McLaren F1. McLaren claims the car will have a top speed of 217.5mph and will reach 186mph in under 17 seconds. The P1 is believed to be capable of speeds nearing 239 mph, but the car will be electronically limited to 217 mph. Acceleration from a standing start means that the P1 can hit 60mph in under three seconds and hits 186mph (300kmh) in under 17 seconds.

With a powertrain that uses technology and know-how from Formula One, the P1 will be powered by a revised version of the 3.8-litre twin-turbo V8 petrol engine used in the McLaren MP4-12C, tuned to 727bhp.

The engine will work in tandem with a 176bhp Kinetic Energy Regeneration System (KERS) similar to the kinds used in F1 that recover power that would otherwise be lost while braking. This hybrid powertrain is connected to a seven-speed dual-clutch transmission and, combined, will mean the P1 has a total power output of just over 900bhp at 7500 rpm and a maximum torque figure of 900Nm – figures that are virtually unmatched outside the rarest of hypercar exotica.

The powertrain can run using either the petrol V8 by itself or with the electric motor. Like mainstream hybrid road cars, electrical power is stored in batteries and the P1 can be charged via plug-in equipment. Unlike road cars the stored energy can be used to deliver a KERS-like boost in performance; an Instant Power Assist System will provide an instant boost to the petrol engine via the electric motor.

Another F1 innovation will be a Drag Reduction System (DRS), which operates the car's rear wing to eliminate downforce in straight lines. Carbon-ceramic brakes provide stopping power and styling will largely be influenced by the McLaren MP4-12C supercar, with a carbon fibre monocoque and roof structure safety cage concept called MonoCage.

Four driving modes will be selectable – normal, sport, track and race – while the whole suspension can be raised by 50mm at speeds of up to 37mph for city driving.

No more than 375 cars will be produced, all fully equipped for road and track. Every model will cost in excess of $1m and the car will battle against LaFerrari for mainstream hypercar supremacy.

SPECIFICATION

MANUFACTURE DATE	2013	ENGINE	McLaren M838T twin-turbo 3.8 L V8 with KERS facility
WIDTH	2,946 mm	TRANSMISSION	Seven-speed dual-clutch
HEIGHT	1,170 mm	0-62 MPH	3.0 seconds
LENGTH	4,585 mm	POWER OUTPUT	727 / bhp
MAXIMUM TORQUE	900 / nm	BRAKES	Le Mans-spec 390mm front brake discs with six-piston calipers, and 380mm rear brakes with four-piston calipers
MAXIMUM SPEED	217 mph	SUSPENSION	Nitrogen-filled carbon-fibre accumulator self-levelling system

SALEEN
S7 TWIN TURBO

The Saleen S7 Twin Turbo has headline-grabbing performance statistics including a top speed of 248mph.
For a car to reach such frightening speeds it takes an incredibly powerful engine and engineering brilliance and the Saleen S7 Twin Turbo can claim to have both.

The engine is a 7.0-litre V8 originally used in the first Saleen S7 but the addition of twin turbochargers has boosted power from around 500bhp to 750bhp and 952Nm of torque at 4800rpm. Developed in-house, the engine is matched to a six-speed manual transmission.

When coupled with a kerbweight of just 1,338kg the Saleen S7 Twin Turbo delivers phenomenal performance to take the title of fastest US production car ever built.

The Saleen S7 Twin turbo can accelerate from 0-62mph in less than three seconds and goes on to hit 100mph in less than six seconds. Formidable performance calls for advanced technology and the Saleen S7 uses specially-designed Brembo brakes and diffusers and spoilers to increase down force.

The Saleen S7 Twin Turbo has its origins in Ford's most iconic car, the Mustang. Famed Mustang engineer Steve Saleen is behind the creation of the US' fastest production car and even uses a Ford NASCAR engine for his supercar.

The large brakes and power-assisted, rack-and-pinion steering are a supercar driver's dream; they enable the car to be precise around corners with sharp, corrective handling wherever necessary in order to keep the car on the road.

Striking scissor doors and a traditional, low, curvaceous supercar shape will appeal to supercar enthusiasts almost as much as the Saleen S7's driving characteristics.

Meanwhile the interior includes some luxury touches including leather and aluminium highlights, custom luggage as standard and a rear view camera to make up for low visibility in the rear.

The rear-wheel drive supercar is significantly less expensive than its supercar rivals, despite offering performance and torque figures that cannot be matched by some of the big players from the likes of Ferrari and Lamborghini.

So performance-oriented is the two-door supercar that a racing version, named the Saleen S7R designed to compete in the Le Mans series.

SPECIFICATION

MANUFACTURE DATE	2005 - 2009	ENGINE	7.0-litre V8 petrol
WIDTH	1,990 mm	TRANSMISSION	Six-speed manual
HEIGHT	1,041 mm	0-62 MPH	2.9 seconds
LENGTH	4,774 mm	POWER OUTPUT	750 / bhp
MAXIMUM TORQUE	925 / nm	BRAKES	Brembo disc brakes
MAXIMUM SPEED	248 mph	SUSPENSION	Double-wishbone suspension with aluminium dampers and anti-roll bar

LOTEC
SIRIUS

When small German supercar manufacturer Lotec announced the Sirius would be as quick as some of the fastest cars in the world there were a few raised eyebrows.

However, the use of a Mercedes-derived 6.0-litre V12 engine taken from a Pagani Zonda enabled Lotec to push the Sirius on to a top speed of 248mph.

Not only did Lotec take the engine from one of the fastest hypercars in existence it also added two turbochargers to the engine to boost power to 1183bhp and 1320Nm of torque at 3400rpm.

The lightweight design of the Lotec, which weighs just 1280kg, means it boasts one of the most impressive power-to-weight ratios in the world at 925bhp per ton. The weight is helped by a carbon fiber body, the material used in many of the world's fastest cars because of its lightweight design and strength during impact.

Despite the top speed approaching 250mph and incredible torque, the car is slightly slower than the likes of the Bugatti Veyron to reach 62mph at 3.8 seconds.

The Lotec Sirius is a car that is sold in exceptionally small numbers worldwide. Owner Lotec is perhaps better known for improving the performance of Mercedes cars instead of venturing into the world of supercar production.

High prices and low availability mean that seeing a Lotec Sirius on the road is extremely rare but its distinctive strip, headlamps and wrap-around windscreen and rear window are great styling touches. The company is capable of producing just five cars per year and as a result this is an extremely rare car.

Other features are taken from supercar royalty including a six-speed manual CIMA gearbox taken from the Pagani Zonda and the dashboard from the Porsche 944 Turbo.

The Lotec Sirius comes with a high level of equipment considering its hypercar performance and standard features include air conditioning, power steering and sports bucket seats with three-point harnesses.

SPECIFICATION

MANUFACTURE DATE	2009	ENGINE	6.0-litre V12 petrol
WIDTH	2,080 mm	TRANSMISSION	Six-speed manual CIMA gearbox
HEIGHT	1,120 mm	0-62 MPH	3.8 seconds
LENGTH	4,120 mm	POWER OUTPUT	1,183 / bhp
MAXIMUM TORQUE	1,320 / nm	BRAKES	4 ram AP IMSA racing brakes
MAXIMUM SPEED	248 mph	SUSPENSION	Unequal- length Double-wishbone with anti-roll bar

DAUER PORSCHE
962
LE MANS

With only 13 Dauer Porsche 962 Le Mans road cars ever built it's one of the more rare supercars on the planet, though it's certainly one of the more recognisable.

One of a number of supercars that started life as a prototype racecar, it was developed from a stripped-down Porsche 962 chassis. The Dauer 962 Le Mans replaced some body panels with carbon fiber and kevlar, while the underbody tray was flattened to boost stability at high speeds.

An adjustable hydraulic suspension system, a second seat, leather trim and a small luggage compartment were added to the road cars, but the cabin remained simple and smart rather than sumptuous. A video screen for DVD playback was added to later models.

The engine is a 2994cc water-cooled, twin-cam, four-valves Porsche flat-six strapped to a pair of turbochargers capable of developing 730bhp at 7,400rpm. That means from a standing start the 0-60mph sprint takes just 2.6 seconds in first gear – with double that speed taking around five seconds. The transmission used the normal 962 manual box and clutch through Tiptronic knobs on the steering wheel.

Although the Dauer Porsche 962 Le Mans was officially claimed to achieve 230 mph, there are unverified claims that the car could exceeded 250 mph. At 1080kg, the 962 Le Mans has a power-to weight ratio superior to the McLaren F1 – the car was claimed to be the fastest road-legal production car in the world in the mid-90s.

SPECIFICATION

MANUFACTURE DATE	1984	ENGINE	2,994 cc Porsche flat 6 twin turbo
WIDTH	1,985 mm	TRANSMISSION	Five-speed manual RWD
HEIGHT	1,050 mm	0-62 MPH	2.6 seconds
LENGTH	4,650 mm	POWER OUTPUT	730 / bhp @ 7,400 rpm
MAXIMUM TORQUE	700 / nm @ 5,000 rpm	BRAKES	330mm Brembo ventilated discs with 4-piston calipers
MAXIMUM SPEED	230mph	SUSPENSION	Double-wishbone suspension with adjustable anti-roll bars

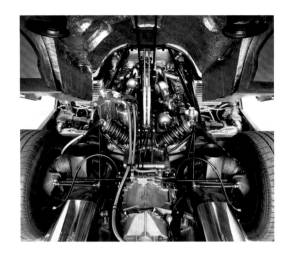

BUGATTI
VEYRON

The car that re-started the fastest production car cold war, the Bugatti Veyron boasts a top speed of 253 mph, making it the fastest production car ever built when it hit the streets in 2006.

That the Veyron originated in the Volkswagen Group was also notable, with the title of fastest production car being tilted at by numerous examples of low-volume exotica in the years preceding the Bugatti hypercar.

The Veyron took the title from the McLaren F1 – for a long time the last word in high-speed road cars – and hung on to it until superseded by an even faster version of the same model – the Super Sport.

The Veyron outputs 987bhp and is good for a top speed of 253mph courtesy of a quad-turbocharged 8-litre WR16 with peak torque of 1250Nm developed between 2200 and 5500rpm.

Creating all that power and torque was one thing, but transmitting it to the Veyron's four wheels required a bespoke transmission, resulting in a seven-speed twin-clutch DSG gearbox operated automatically or via paddle shifters, with lightning-quick changes thanks to the presence of two clutches, one engaged and one waiting to be engaged.

Torque is split automatically depending on conditions and, at 137mph, the Veyron lowers its suspension and extends a rear spoiler to increase downforce. To push onto the top speed the driver must switch on a different driving mode that turns off these aids and ensure that tyres are undamaged. The result is decreased downforce and a slipper drag coefficient, enabling the top speed of 253mph.

To 200mph from a standing start takes 22 seconds and the standing quarter-mile a mere 10.8 seconds. The Veyron remains a technological marvel – one that doesn't offer a stripped-out interior without everyday usability but is perfectly pliable as a grand tourer – and will continue to be synonymous with the title of fastest production car.

SPECIFICATION

MANUFACTURE DATE	2006-2011	ENGINE	Quad-turbocharged and intercooled DOHC 64-valve 7998cc W-16, aluminium block and heads, direct fuel injection
WIDTH	1,998 mm	TRANSMISSION	Seven-speed manual with automated shifting and clutch
HEIGHT	1,159 mm	0-62 MPH	2.9 seconds
LENGTH	4,462 mm	POWER OUTPUT	987 / bhp @ 6,000 rpm
MAXIMUM TORQUE	1,250 / nm @ 2,200 rpm	BRAKES	Carbon-ceramic eight-piston, four-pad calipers at front; six-piston, two-pad calipers at rear
MAXIMUM SPEED	253 mph	SUSPENSION	Independent Double-wishbone Front & Rear

KOENIGSEGG
CCXR

The Koenigsegg CCXR was an ultra-low-volume biofuel roadster released in 2008 with enough power and top speed to bother the Bugatti Veyron, then the official fastest production car.

The performance statistic are quite fascinating. With a relatively small-displacement 4.8-litre engine boosted by two centrifugal superchargers the CCXR was capable of a reported 254mph, developing 1,018bhp and sprinting to 60mph in 2.9 seconds when using bioethanol. A standing start to 124mph and back again took just 13.5 seconds.

One of the secrets of the Koenigsegg hypercar is that it is clothed almost completely in lightweight carbon fiber and boasts other weight-saving trickery as an aluminium honeycomb chassis and hollow drive shafts, but the performance improvements offered by higher-octane bioethanol meant that more power could be wrung from the engine due to the higher cylinder pressures that the cooling properties of the fuel allowed.

With all that power, came the need for plenty of downforce. As a result the CCXR came with an adjustable rear wing and massive front splitter. Meanwhile ceramic disc brakes, a limited-slip differential and five-mode traction control ensured the car stayed in contact with the tarmac.

The CCXR didn't skimp either. Leather carpets, a DVD player, satellite navigation and a rear-view parking camera were among standard offerings. The Koenigsegg's glass roof was removable too.

The CCXR wasn't just fast – in a world of petrol-powered coupés and as a biofuel drop-top, it offered something genuinely different.

SPECIFICATION

MANUFACTURE DATE	2007–2011	ENGINE	4759cc, V8 petrol / bioethanol
WIDTH	1,996 mm	TRANSMISSION	Six-speed sequential
HEIGHT	1,120 mm	0-62 MPH	2.9 seconds
LENGTH	4,293 mm	POWER OUTPUT	1,018 / bhp @ 7,200 rpm
MAXIMUM TORQUE	1,060 / nm @ 5,600 rpm	BRAKES	380mm power-assisted front ventilated ceramic disc brakes with 8-piston light alloy Brembo calipers at front; 362mm power-assisted rear ventilated ceramic disc brakes with 6-piston light alloy AP Racing calipers at rear
MAXIMUM SPEED	254mph	SUSPENSION	Double-wishbone, two-way adjustable VPS gas-hydraulic shock absorbers, pushrod operated

9FF
GT9

The fastest-ever Porsche-based supercar is
the 9ff GT9, a coupé built by tuning company
9ff that uses the Porsche 911 997 GT3 as
donor car and produces the 254mph GT9.
So heavily modified from the original was the
GT9 that it reputedly shared only two per cent
of the same components with the 911 GT3.

The 911 GT3 body was stretched by 300mm and flattened
by 120mm to maximize downforce at high speeds.
Meanwhile heavy use of carbon-fiber and Kevlar meant
the GT9 weighed in at a lightweight 1,326kg.

The models use a heavily-modified 4.0-litre flat-six petrol engine
mounted in the middle of the car, as opposed to the traditional
rear position for which the 911 is famous.

The engine is capable of developing 987bhp and a top speed of
254mph, making it faster than the Bugatti Veyron. 0-60mph took
2.9 seconds and 0-190mph less than 16 seconds.

Very much a racing car, the 911's interior was stripped out to make the GT9, with blue leather trim and a roll cage added. Neither traction control nor stability control were available with the GT9, ensuring the coupé attracted only hardcore – and well-to-do at around $800,000 – buyers.

Only 20 of the most powerful models were ever sold, making the GT9 one of the most exclusive fastest cars on the planet.

SPECIFICATION

MANUFACTURE DATE	2007–2008	ENGINE	4.0-litre B6 twin-turbo
WIDTH	1,860 mm	TRANSMISSION	Six-speed Manual
HEIGHT	1,180 mm	0-62 MPH	2.9 seconds
LENGTH	4,733 mm	POWER OUTPUT	987 / bhp
MAXIMUM TORQUE	964 / nm	BRAKES	Ceramic brake system; 2-piece brake discs with aluminium bells; 380mm 6-piston brake calipers at front; 350 4-piston brake calipers at rear
MAXIMUM SPEED	254 mph	SUSPENSION	Fully adjustable suspension with adjustable aluminium shock absorbers

BUGATTI VEYRON
16.4 GRAND SPORT VITESSE

The Bugatti Veyron 16.4 Grand Sport Vitesse promised to unite the elegance of the Grand Sport and the performance of the Super Sport – it remains the fastest production roadster ever built as of 2013 and an incredible feat of engineering in its own right.

An improved version of the eight-litre W16 engine is capable of developing maximum torque of 1,500Nm between 3,000–5,000rpm and provides maximum power of 1,184bhp at 6,400rpm.

Those awesome figures mean the Vitesse can cover the sprint in just 2.6 seconds and go on to a top speed of 255mph, with power transmitted through a new version of the 7-speed DSG dual-clutch transmission. Such is the quantity of fuel being burned at maximum speed that the waste heat from the Veyron's engine could warm ten family homes in the winter.

Powering a car to over 250mph requires a delicate balance between aerodynamic slipperiness and downforce to ensure traction – the Veyron's mix of suspension settings and aerodynamic features ensures that the car is stable at 250mph.

However, removing the Veyron's roof obviously compromises this balance. As a result the front end of the Grand Sport Vitesse is characterized by larger air intakes and the rear characterized by a double diffuser and a centrally-positioned twin tailpipe.

Removing the roof also poses certain torsional stiffness differences, so a full carbon fiber monocoque ensures stiffness of 22,000Nm per degree. A third problem with producing a roadster capable of over 250mph is the issue of tyre and wind noise so engineers added a new, stowable, windbreak that Bugatti promised would ensure relaxed open-top driving even at a speed illegal in most countries.

That the Vitesse can manage that top speed at all is astounding. That it can do it as a roadster just makes the Veyron – already an incredible car – that much more astonishing.

SPECIFICATION

MANUFACTURE DATE	2006-2011	ENGINE	Quad-turbocharged and intercooled DOHC 64-valve 7998cc W-16, aluminium block and heads, direct fuel injection
WIDTH	1,998 mm	TRANSMISSION	Seven-speed manual with automated shifting and clutch
HEIGHT	1,159 mm	0-62 MPH	2.6 seconds
LENGTH	4,462 mm	POWER OUTPUT	1,184 / bhp
MAXIMUM TORQUE	1,500 / nm	BRAKES	Carbon-ceramic eight-piston, four-pad calipers at front; six-piston, two-pad calipers at rear
MAXIMUM SPEED	255 mph	SUSPENSION	Independent Double-wishbone Front & Rear

HENNESSEY
VENOM GT

The Hennessey Venom GT may not quite be the world's fastest production car, but it is the world's fastest accelerating production car – capable of going to 186mph (300km/h) in 13.63 seconds.

Not only that it went on to claim an unofficial 0-200mph time of 14.51 seconds – beating the likes of the Koenigsegg Agera R by over three seconds and the Bugatti Veyron by more than seven seconds. It's a fast car.

The Venom GT is hardly a slouch in the top speed stakes either; capable of 260mph it's among the elite fastest cars in the world - company founder John Hennessey claims the Venom is, in fact, the fastest production car available to the public as the Veyron's record-breaking runs have been achieved with a speed-limiter deactivated.

Powered by a 7.0-litre V8 producing 1,244 hp and 1,565Nm of torque, the two-seater, real-wheel-drive coupé weighs just 1,244kg – meaning a power-to-weight ratio of exactly one horsepower per kilogram of kerbweight.

The Venom GT is loosely based on the chassis of a Lotus Exige, with extensive modifications and various driver aids to ensure traction. A programmable traction control system manages power output, with power adjustable by the driver so that bands of 800bhp, 1000bhp and the maximum power of 1244bhp are available.

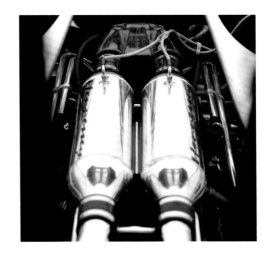

An active aero system with an adjustable rear wing deploys at very high speeds, increasing downforce, while an adjustable suspension system will allow ride height adjustments according to speed and driving conditions.

With Hennessey only planning to build 29 Venom GTs at a rate of one a year and over $1m each – not to mention with a stereo system supposedly designed by Steven Tyler of Aerosmith – the Venom GT is likely to remain a highly sought-after piece of hypercar exotica.

SPECIFICATION

MANUFACTURE DATE	20012	ENGINE	Chevrolet LS V8 Block 6.2 Litre with twin Garrett ball-bearing turbochargers
WIDTH	1,960 mm	TRANSMISSION	Ricardo Six-speed Manual
HEIGHT	1,079 mm	0-62 MPH	2.9 seconds
LENGTH	4,655 mm	POWER OUTPUT	1,244 / bhp
MAXIMUM TORQUE	1,565 / nm	BRAKES	Brembo 6-piston on carbon ceramic discs
MAXIMUM SPEED	260 mph	SUSPENSION	Type: KW Variant 3 Adjustable Coilover

KOENIGSEGG
AGERA R

The Agera R made its debut at the March 2011 Geneva Motor Show trumpeted as a supercar capable of running on biofuel – something Koenigsegg has shown in the past with the CCX.

The Agera R can accelerate from to 60mph in 2.9 seconds and reach a theoretical top speed of approximately 275mph, though it is officially rated at 260mph. During testing the Agera R managed to rack up a Guinness World Records for high-speed acceleration and braking in a two-seater production car 0-300-0 km/h in 21.19 seconds.

The Koenigsegg hypercar is powered by a 1,115bhp 5.0-litre V8 twin-turbo petrol engine. Power is transmitted through a dual clutch transmission for faster gearshifts.

The Agera has a body made from pre-impregnated carbon fiber and Kevlar with lightweight reinforcements., while the chassis is made using carbon fiber with an aluminium honeycomb.

The Agera comes with forged aluminium wheels with centre locking and a set of Michelin Super Sport tyres good for 260mph. Unlike some hypercars, there's a traction control system, while the active wing on the Agera R balances downforce and aerodynamic slippiness.

It's manually or automatically adjustable – in the latter case it uses the pressure of the wind created at high speeds to force the wing downward and reduce wind resistance – meaning it is lighter than conventional hydraulics and instantly adaptable to headwinds or tailwinds.

Other highlights include the trademark Koenigsegg right-angle doors and a custom interior with Ghost Light lighting system, which uses carbon nanotubes to backlight the car's aluminium buttons. Koenigsegg claims the Agera R has the largest trunk space of any hypercar at 120 litres, where the roof can be stowed if topless driving is desired.

With those everyday touches the Agera R almost becomes a new kind of car entirely – a hypercar GT.

SPECIFICATION

MANUFACTURE DATE	2012	ENGINE	5.0-litre V8 with twin turbos
WIDTH	1,996 mm	TRANSMISSION	Seven-speed dual clutch
HEIGHT	1,120 mm	0-62 MPH	2.8 seconds
LENGTH	4,293 mm	POWER OUTPUT	1,115 / bhp
MAXIMUM TORQUE	1,200 / nm	BRAKES	392mm and 380mm ventilated and drilled ceramic discs
MAXIMUM SPEED	260 mph	SUSPENSION	Koenigsegg Triplex suspension

KOENIGSEGG // AGERA R

FAST CARS
FASTEST
CAR IN THE WORLD

BUGATTI
VEYRON SUPER SPORT

Where do you go from the fastest ever production car? If you're Bugatti you go even faster. The Veyron Super Sport was first unveiled in 2010 and immediately became the world's fastest production car, courtesy of its 267.856mph top speed.

Despite queries over the validity of the claim given the production car's speed limiter, which brings the attainable speed down to a mere 258mph, the Guinness Book of World Records still proclaims the Super Sport the fastest car in the world as of 2013.

With a power increase to 1,188bhp, torque boost to 1,500Nm and aerodynamic tweaks, the grand tourer is capable of 267mph, but is limited to 258mph to prevent its tyres from overheating. However it does cover the 60mph sprint in 2.5 seconds dead and 124mph (200km/h) in 6.7 seconds.

Because the sheer power required to move at those speeds through air increases exponentially with every mile-per-hour, the Super Sport will empty its 100-litre fuel tank in eight minutes when travelling at top speed, as opposed to the standard Veyron managing to burn through its fuel in 12.

The Veyron represents the very limits of our grasp of physics; sending a car that can happily admit two people and an air conditioning unit at speeds well beyond what's possible for a Formula One car.

As a mark of how difficult that is, Bugatti is believed to lose money on every Veyron it sells – the sheer weight of research and development required means an outlay of many millions of dollars.

30 will be produced at prices of over $2m. Chances are you might never even see one. The best car in the world? Perhaps. But the Bugatti Veyron Super Sports is certainly the fastest.

SPECIFICATION

MANUFACTURE DATE	2011	ENGINE	Quad-turbocharged and intercooled DOHC 64-valve 7998cc W-16, aluminium block and heads, direct fuel injection
WIDTH	1,998 mm	TRANSMISSION	Seven-speed manual with automated shifting and clutch
HEIGHT	1,159 mm	0-62 MPH	2.5 seconds
LENGTH	4,462 mm	POWER OUTPUT	1,188 / bhp
MAXIMUM TORQUE	1,500 / nm	BRAKES	Carbon-ceramic eight-piston, four-pad calipers at front; six-piston, two-pad calipers at rear
MAXIMUM SPEED	267 mph	SUSPENSION	Independent Double-wishbone Front & Rear

FAST CARS
INDEX

PICTURE CREDITS